NATIVE BRITISH TREES

by

Andy Thompson

with additional illustrations by

Lucy Phillips

I would like to dedicate this book to my wife Annie and family and would also like to thank Lucy Philips and John Martineau for their help and support in the production of this small directory of native trees.

Should the reader be interested I would like to suggest the following titles: Roger Phillips "Trees in Europe and North America" (1978), Oliver Rackham "Trees and Woodland in the British Landscape" (1976) and J. Edward Milner "The Tree Book" (1992).

Most of the illustrations have been taken from John Evelyn's "Silva" (1776) and from Mattioli's "Commentaries on the Six Books of Dioscorides" (1563).

First published 1998 AD
© Wooden Books Ltd 2005 AD

Published by Wooden Books Ltd.
12A High St, Glastonbury, Somerset

British Library Cataloguing in Publication Data
Thompson, A. 1963–
Native British Trees

A CIP catalogue record for this little book
is available from the British Library

ISBN 1 904263 32 1

Printed and bound in Great Britain
by The Cromwell Press,
Trowbridge, Wiltshire, UK.

CONTENTS

Wild Pear – Pyrus pyraster

A rather rare pyramidal tree that can grow to 60', often with thorny
branches. It needs a warmer climate than the Apple (*see page 36*) and
favours light deep soils. The Pear's white flowers produce roundedfruits
which are readily eaten by birds and forest animals.

# INTRODUCTION

Trees are such a prominent feature of the landscape and yet we tend to take them for granted. They have provided shade from the sun and shelter from the wind and rain, they manufacture life-giving oxygen with their leaves, enrich the soil and provide food and shelter for a great variety of wildlife.

They have provided man with some of his most valuable construction materials, kept him warm, fed him with nuts and fruits, nursed him with medicines and calmed his spirits with their beauty and grace.

The last ice age cleared our shores of tree-life. As the ice receded our native trees returned to cover a large proportion of the land. These trees include all that are mentioned in this book - Sweet Chestnut has been included as it has grown in Britain for over 2000 years. All the other trees now growing in Britain were intro-duced by man either for ornament, timber or their fruit.

Overleaf are listed the more common introduced species with an approximate arrival date.

Sycamore	*acer pseudoplatanus*	c. 1250
Walnut	*juglans regia*	c. 1400
Plane	*platanus orientalis*	c. 1580
Fir	*abies sp.*	c. 1600
Horse chestnut	*aesculus hippocastanum*	c. 1600
Larch	*larix decidua*	c. 1629

Cedars and Sequoias did not arrive until the 18th century passion for collecting exotic plants came to the fore. Trees at this time started to take a more important role in the landscape – not just as boundary markers but as landscape design features.

The continued survival of our trees is dependent on man's ability to gain profit from them. Commercially, they survive as plantations and woodlands, where they provide a most valuable resource, harvested by either coppicing (cutting and allowing to re-shoot from the stump), or felling and replanting. This way they supply us with wood for chairs to sit on and houses to live in, as well as material of infinite variety to create items of immense beauty, style and colour.

Throughout time trees have kept us warm and reference has been made in these pages to the burning quality of each species – a warm fire is good for body and soul, a damp smoky one doing little for either.

Charcoal (created by partial burning with restricted oxygen to create a high temperature fuel) is also mentioned, and was an essential ingredient of our industrial development. Huge acreages of woodland with suitable species were managed solely to produce charcoal for smelting metals. It is now mostly used as a smokeless cooking fuel for barbecues, other uses are noted in the book.

As a landscape feature trees provide us with aesthetic profit, be it a lone Pine on the skyline or a well designed multi-level woodland with vistas and viewpoints, colour and atmosphere, where we can relax or contemplate. They transform our urban drabness with their shade, colour and habitat and as such will always be revered by us.

Cascob, Powys

ASH
Fraxinus excelsior

King of trees to the Vikings with its roots in hell and its branches reaching to the heavens (120'+), the solo Ash tree will rarely blow over.

Last to come into leaf and first to fall with dappled shade, Ash woodland supports a rich ground flora.

An awkward tree to climb, Ash will tolerate pruning well and has been successfully pollarded and coppiced for centuries. Its amazing speed of growth causes its timber to be tough and flexible, sawing and seasoning well when winter felled.

It is used in vehicle construction, tool handles and sports equipment.

The queen of firewood trees, clean Ash splits easily (a hazard when felling) and burns even when green.

OAK
Quercus robur / petrea

The Oak is our most common broadleaved tree and has been the most dominant timber tree since earliest times. The two British species are closely related and can hybridise. The flowers appear in early May, followed by the leaves. The familiar acorns occur in autumn with great numbers being produced every six or seven years after a suitable preceding spring.

The tree often has a second flush of leaves known as Llamas growth which helps it to recover from the almost totally defoliating attacks of caterpillars in some years. The Oak supports the widest variety of insect and other invertebrate life (including fungi) of any species in the British Isles.

The timber is widely used in building, fencing, joinery and boatbuilding and is extremely durable. Its bark peeled in spring is used for tanning high quality leather.

A slow burning firewood it produces the best charcoal for swordsmithing.

ELM
Ulmus glabra / procera

Elms are large, shady classically shaped trees. They essentially fall into two lowland species (often naturally hybridised) and until the mid 1970's they were one of the most abundant trees of the British countryside.

The Dutch Elm plague has now removed all the major trees bar a few hidden in the sheltered valleys of Wales and Scotland. Regeneration from the profuse sucker growth may yet prove the key to its survival - this once major player came back from near extinction 5000 years ago.

Its large bole yields superb timber. It is highly prized for although sawn easily it resists splitting and so became favoured for wheel hubs, chair bottoms, coffin boards and such like. Underwater, elm lasts indefinitely and used to be used for boat bottoms, pipes and piles.

Elm charcoal made from seasoned wood has many medicinal properties. The inner bark of the fresh-felled tree can be prepared as food and is useful for stomach upsets.

A poor firewood until completely dry.

BEECH
Fagus sylvatica

Much planted and widespread. Solo trees develop huge canopies with dense shade beneath. Classic Beech woodland is clean underfoot as the trees are so effective at collecting the sunlight. Top quality leaf mould is formed on the wood floor.

Shallow rooted, the major Beech trees are in decline with lowering water tables causing premature die-back of the biggest, and storm winds claiming many others.

The bright green spring leaves are good to eat but not so the later dark green leaves.

Beech timber is close grained, hard and strong. It is very heavy when felled. A classic furniture wood with a tendency to 'move' it is usually used in smaller components - chairlegs, steam-bent backs etc. An excellent flooring material rich in colour and hard wearing.

Young Beech will burn green but well seasoned it produces a lovely bright fire.

HORNBEAM
Carpinus betulus

A medium sized, rounded tree, similar to Beech, but with serrated edged leaves, older trees having a twisted, fluted bole.

Hornbeam is more common in the south where it was highly valued and managed most often by pollarding. It tolerates hard pruning well and is useful as garden hedging as it grows well in partial shade.

The wood is very heavy and strong. The name "Hornbeam" originates from its use in oxen yokes – the beam between the horns. The timber's resistance to wear made it useful for cogs in machinery, pulleys, mallets, chopping blocks and certain piano components.

Sometimes known as candlewood it makes a bright fire when seasoned and a good quality charcoal.

CHESTNUT
Castanea sativa

Introduced in Roman times from Mediterranean lands this much loved tree can now almost be treated as native; often a large tree attaining 100' with a large trunk with grey bark deeply furrowed and most often spiralled.

After a long dry summer large trees can crop many delicious chestnuts for roasting.

Extensively coppiced, the durable smallwood has found a variety of uses from paling, fencing and walking sticks to hop-poles. Large trees yield superb if bland timber as good as Oak in all but looks.

Being subject to both ring-shake and ink-spot disease, and being intolerant of lime, the tree is less common in the west and grows smaller in the north of Britain.

A poor firewood that spits, it none the less makes good charcoal that kindles well.

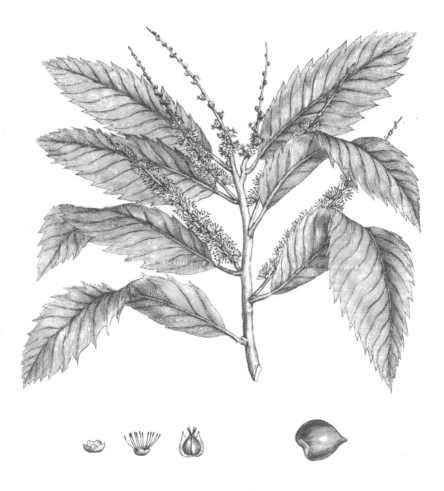

15

LIME
Tilia cordata / platyphyllos

Two species of Lime, the small-leaved (*cordata*) and the large-leaved (*platyphyllos*), are native to Britain. The small-leaved Lime used to be wider spread than it is today. More common now is their hybrid which can occur naturally but is more usually from imported Dutch stock.

Once the major component of the wild wood Limes are amongst the longest living and tallest (around 130 feet) of our native trees.

Heavily scented flowers open in late June and are loved by bees who often become 'drunk' on their nectar. They are also host to the Lime aphid that produces the sticky honey-dew so hated by motorists.

Tolerant of hard pruning, Lime was once widely coppiced and is now often subjected to severe lopping as a management technique when used as a street tree.

Lime wood being soft and even-grained is ideal for carving and, as it doesn't warp, is still used for the sounding boards in pianos.

It forms a bright fire and charcoals well.

MAPLE
Acer campestre

The Field Maple is a round-headed tree with a sinuous pale grey trunk; the ends of its branches droop down then turn up and the stalk of the delicate lobed leaf exudes a milky substance when   broken off.

Occurring in woodlands and hedgerows particularly on warmer soils it tolerates cutting hard and is often found as hedging.

Traditionally widely coppiced, although also grown as a standard tree, Maple wood is fine grained and brown and much loved by wood turners as it can be worked very thinly. It is also made into veneers with Birds-Eye Maple being cut from burred logs. Maple has long been the favoured wood for harps.

Good firewood was often produced by pollarding and maple syrup can be extracted in the spring.

Maples add a fantastic orange glow to the treescape in autumn.

19

BIRCH
Betula pubescens / verucosa

There are two main species that can be classed as one.

Most liked by those who look at it, the white bark and striking foliage, pale green in spring and yellow in autumn, have inspired many landscape painters.

A primary coloniser, it can grow on the poorest of soils and spread like wild-fire. Although still considered a 'weed' by many foresters the Birch is now enjoying favour from conservationists as it establishes itself so easily and supports a highly diverse fauna.

The 'witches-broom' plant-gall is caused by fungus and often inhabits more mature birch trees.

Birch timber was used when no other was available although it is as tough as Ash and suitable for turnery and utensils. Besom brooms and brushwood horse jumps ensure it is still coppiced a-plenty. Older trees do not tolerate hard pruning.

Birch sap tapped in early April is used to make a unique tasting wine.

When burnt the logs form a quick bright fire.

ELDER
Sambucus nigra

A small tree, frequently branching close to the base and flourishing wherever the nitrogen content of the soil is high, near dwellings and refuse heaps. Interestingly, flies have an aversion to the leaves which if dried and powdered make a useful insect repellent.

Elder colonises very quickly and soon becomes established, often under timber trees including Larch. It is usually cut out of hedgerows during laying as it tends to kill other species with its vigour and shading.

Much loved by children who relish its twigs' soft pith to hollow out for pea-shooters, pipes and whistles.

Easily distinguished by its umbels of highly scented white flowers which, if picked in full sun, make an excellent white wine. A superb claret-like red wine can be made from the abundant purple berries. The berries are rich in vitamin C if a trifle sour and when mixed with honey make an excellent cough remedy.

Strongly associated with evil and never to be burned in a charcoal maker's kiln it is inevitably a lousy firewood.

WHITEBEAM
Sorbus aria

The Whitebeam is a small tree 30-50' tall. A light-demanding, warmth-loving species it is often found on chalk or limestone hills facing south, although the attractive appearance and ability to thrive in urban and heavily polluted enviroments has led to its being widely planted in recent years.

From spring onwards the white down beneath the surprisingly large leaves decks the tree in silver. Sweet-scented white flowers appear in May, then red berries much loved by birds and squirrels occur with the golden leaves of autumn.

Overripe berries were made into jelly to accompany venison whilst the timber, although small, being white and fine-grained was valued for wood-turning and fine joinery.

When dry the wood burns slowly.

WILD SERVICE
Sorbus torminalis

One of the rarest of Britain's native trees, the Wild Service is generally a small to medium sized tree with a wide crown and leaves like a maple both in shape and autumn colouring. In May it is covered in thick white blossom.

Cracks form in the bark peeling off into squares, leading to the tree also being known as the Chequers Tree. It has small brown exotically flavoured berries that used to be picked ripe in September then hung outside to sweeten in frosts before being eaten. The berries were also a well-known cure for dysentry and colic.

Regarded as an indicator of ancient woodland it is now much less widespread because of its slow growth and poor germination, although in certain sites it can sucker profusely.

The wood is heavy and hard and was used for carving and for making rulers, gauges and instrument components.

Wild Service is not to be encouraged as firewood due to its rarity, slow regrowth and unsuitability to coppice management.

ROWAN
Sorbus aucuparia

A familiar and graceful tree, often known as Mountain Ash. Of medium size with ascending branches it produces an ovoid crown.

The white flowers appear in May and develop into pea-sized orange-red berries in the autumn which when eaten by wild birds ensure the tree's widespread dispersal. The berries, once used by bird catchers to bait their traps, can be made into a delicious jelly rich in vitamin C.

Connected with witchcraft from ancient times the tree was often planted outside houses and churchyards to ward off witches.

A common element of many hedgerows, it responds well to coppicing, producing useful small poles.

The Rowan's strong, flexible, yellow-grey wood was used widely for making tool handles and small carved objects.

Poor firewood.

HAZEL
Corylus avellana

Hazel was one of the first trees to grow in these islands soon after the last ice age. A common component of hedgerows, it tolerates shade well and often occurs beneath timber trees in Oak and Ash woods.

On good soil Hazel can grow into a 35' broad-crowned tree but has been almost universally coppiced to produce its thin flexible rods that have been woven into a variety of products useful to man. Interestingly, hazel products last much longer when made from rods cut in the winter when the sap is down.

It is striking in February when covered in 'lambs tail' catkins that eventually form into delicious nuts usually stripped by the grey squirrels before they ripen.

The best water divining rods are of hazel and larger wood makes fine charcoal and bright firewood.

31

HAWTHORN
Crataegus monogyna

Hawthorn is one of the most common British trees.

A quick-growing hedge plant, yet growing slowly into a tree, its tangled crown makes a favourite habitat for many nesting birds, its sharp thorns offering excellent protection.

In the right location it can be very long lived indeed.

Flowering in May causes it to be known as May or White-thorn and it is considered unlucky to bring the flowers into the house. A short dead prickly branch makes a deadly deterrent for moles when inserted in their tunnels.

The red fruits or haws ripen in September and are a most important bird food as well as being used for jellies and wines.

Hawthorn wood is tough and hard and is used in fine work, veneers, small tool handles and wood engraving.

It makes excellent firewood and charcoal.

BLACKTHORN
Prunus spinosa

This small tree, often occurring as a large shrub, is native throughout Britain, growing on woodland edges and in hedgerows.

Blackthorn's thorny and unapproachable thickets, formed by vigorous suckering, give protection to other flora and fauna within by warding off grazing animals.

Blackthorn is an excellent hedging plant although it is capable of lodging many a septic splinter. Often confused with Hawthorn in winter its bark is smoother and less deeply fissured. A "Blackthorn Winter" is a long one as the trees often blossom in March during cold east winds. The profusion of small white flowers encourage the hedgelayer to press on, as the stems are less brittle at this time.

The wood has light sapwood and purple-brown heart-wood and is used by wood-turners, for walking sticks and rake teeth. The blue-black fruits known as sloes are made into jams and wine, and are also used to improve the flavour of cheap gin.

An excellent firewood. Faggots of thorn brush traditionally baked the sweetest bread.

CRAB APPLE
Malus sylvestris

The Crab Apple is a small tree in the wild reaching a height of about 30'. It has a broad crown and greyish brown bark that peels off in thin scales.

Crab blossom is pinkish and appears in late May developing into small yellowish-red, hard and bitter fruits which can be made into jelly, jam and wine.

The Crab is the original Apple and still continues as a frost resistant dwarfing rootstock for grafting the garden varieties. Readily growing in hedgerows it tolerates hard pruning. A distant relative of the Rose, it actually has thorns, as does the Wild Pear (*see opposite page 1*).

Crab Apple and Wild Pear share many timber characteristics. The woods are hard and fine grained with many uses, including high quality turnery, wood engraving, musical instruments and naturally occurring sculptors' mallets.

They both produce excellent scented firewood.

CHERRY
Prunus avium

A medium-large conical to broad crowned tree usually with a well developed trunk and shiny reddish-brown bark showered in white flowers in April.

Found in woodlands all over, though perhaps giving way to the Bird Cherry (*P. padus*) in the north, Wild Cherry grows surprisingly rapidly and straight, yielding superb hard tight-grained pinkish-brown timber (European mahogany), ideally suited to cabinet making and used in smoking pipes and musical instruments. The burrs and big knots are sought after for turnery, making beautiful, long-lasting, richly coloured items.

Its fruits tend to be bitter but none the less are edible, and often cultivated cherries are grafted on to this rootstock. Although not coppiced in the true sense its abundant suckering ensures it regenerates freely.

An excellent sweet-smelling firewood.

39

ALDER
Alnus glutinosa

Many of our finest rivers are held on course by the round leaved Alders. Fast growing in wet soils, they can soon transform new earthworks and their ability to set seed when young ensures they are widespread.

It was once considered unlucky to cut Alder as the sap colours red. None the less it has long been used by wood-turners and was favoured by clog-makers as it carves so easily. When coppiced it regrows vigourously as long as the freshly cut stools are protected from grazing stock.

Underwater, Alder will last indefinitely making it useful for piling for bridges and jetties.

The even grain of the wood ensures it charcoals totally making superior gunpowder, adding 50 yards range to ships' cannon.

When well seasoned it is a useful firewood and the bark was used to make a cheap black dye.

41

BLACK POPLAR
Poplus nigra

The Black Poplar is one of the rarest and most distinctive native trees. Although easily recognised from afar it is often confused with other poplars. The trees occur naturally in riverside meadows, often leaning, over 100 feet high and 6 feet thick, with deeply ridged bark; the heavy branches grow in arching curves.

Just before the leaves come out in early April the male trees have red catkins known as 'Devils fingers' and it is thought to be unlucky to pick them up.

Despite the abundant seed produced, Black Poplar propagates best from cuttings and many more should be planted. There is a shortage of female trees as cuttings have long been taken from male trees that do not produce the troublesome fluff of the female catkin.

Poplar timber is light and tough; it was traditionally used to line cart bottoms and even build barns in Gloucestershire. Nowadays it is still used as coffin boards, shelving, toys, plywood, pallets and packing cases.

Although poor firewood its open grain allows it to absorb paraffin wax and hence makes excellent matches.

ASPEN
Populus tremula

It is unusual to find an Aspen tree on its own as they are invariably surrounded by abundant suckers which form new trees.

These slightly leaning trees are conical, though becoming broader when mature. They occur all over, although nowhere in really great numbers. Aspen does tend to favour areas that suffer regular spring flooding.

"To tremble like an Aspen" became a common phrase as the long leaf stalks are flattened causing the leaves to quiver and rustle in the wind - apparently showing guilt for Aspens providing the wood for the cross on which Christ was crucified.

As is so often the case it was convenient to spread bad rumours about trees whose timber was deemed inferior, and so the Aspen. Boards are prone to warping and splitting, and the firewood burns disappointingly fast. However, an infusion made from Spring-collected bark has beneficial medical uses.

A fine looking tree not least in autumn with its amber leaves quivering.

WILLOW
Salix

Two main species of willow are known to be native to Britain. The White Willow (*Salix alba*) is the most common tree-sized willow whilst the Crack Willow (*Salix fragilis*) is the familiar pollarded willow that flanks so many of our rivers and streams. The two species hybridise freely, although in practice propagate themselves by shedding limbs which wash down-stream and then root.

Great care must be taken when felling or pollarding Willow trees as the large wood splits and compresses in unusual ways.

Traditionally harvested for winter fodder, basketry and fencing materials, modern hybrids are enjoying great interest as biomass producers, foul-water purifiers and mediums for living sculpture.

The bark of willow can be chewed as a pain-reliever and its charcoal is still appreciated by artists for drawing.

The dry firewood burns brightly yet quickly.

47

SALLOW
Salix caprea/cinera

Sallow is the colloquial name given to the smaller of the willow species (Sally trees).

The Goat and Grey willows are the most common. Typically with round crown shapes with either a short bole or as a spreading bush with rounded leaves, they are more abundant in forests, scrub and hedgerows than any other willow.

Important pioneer trees in forestry, they quickly colonise waste ground and provide excellent grazing for many animals.

One of the shortest lived of our trees it is unusual to find one over 60 years old, although coppice stools can last much longer and pollards longer still.

The commonly known Pussy Willow provides bees with their first feast in springtime, when the male flowers resemble a yellow bouquet.

The soft, light wood was once made into clothes pegs, rake teeth and hatchet handles.

The firewood burns very fast when dry.

HOLLY
Ilex aquifolium

Given space and light Holly can grow into a fine tree up to 80' tall although more often it grows as a small understorey tree and is common in hedgerows. A narrow conical tree when young, it grows more straggly with age, and the leaves become less prickly. Holly forms superb dense hedging when regularly clipped.

The small flowers appear in May and develop into the familiar red berries by November, a good crop being a sign of a good summer past, not, as traditionally believed, the herald of a bad winter to come.

Often spared the woodman's axe for fear of bad luck, it will tolerate hard pruning with the regenerated shoots making excellent horse whips. It was often used for winter fodder in hard times.

Holly wood is dense and white and often used in small pieces for carving, inlays and woodcuts.

Holly burns fantastically, even when green.

SCOTS PINE
Pinus sylvestris

The only large conifer to recolonize these islands after the retreat of the ice age, the Scots Pine now survives naturally in the much depleted Caledonean Forest.

Successfully reintroduced throughout Britain, the great size, distinctive shape and orange colour of the upper bark of the Scots Pine with its evergreen needle foliage and brown cones make it one of our most important landscape trees. Its ability to thrive on the poorest of soils has also helped its return as it produces superb timber being strong yet soft and easily worked.

The trees yield turpentine from their resin, ships' masts in their length and if quickly sawn after felling superb construction timber. Pine was traditionally only felled when the moon was waning to reduce the resinous content.

Pine scent is associated with freshness and the steam created from boiling Pine shoots is said to relieve bronchial congestion. Various healing potions use Pine turpentine as a constituent.

A hot fire can be built with seasoned Pine although it spits badly.

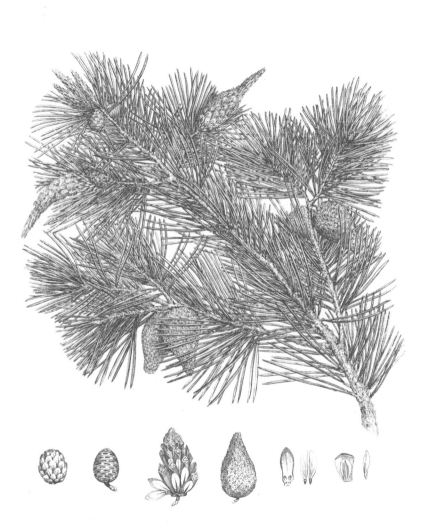

53

JUNIPER
Juniperis communis

The Juniper is one of Britain's native conifers and occurs naturally in the south on chalk downs and in Beech woodland. Further north it grows on limestone moor-land whilst in Scotland it flourishes on the acid soils of the Pine forests.

Often considered a shrub, it has a conical crown when young growing more uneven with age. Distinguished by its red woody stems, dark-hued needle leaves and the blue-black berries that it bears, it can grow to forty feet tall although it will only do so very slowly. The trees can be very long lived.

The famous berries are in fact cones, taking two years to mature, and are used for seasoning food and, of course, flavouring gin. Both the bark and berries can be used medicinally as a tonic and nerve stimulant.

Dry Juniper wood was used for secret fires for illegal stills producing illicit spirits in the Highlands as it produces very little smoke and was traditionally burnt on Halloween to ward off evil.

YEW
Taxus baccata

Our oldest lived, most mysterious and sacred tree. A Yew at Discoed, Powys, is reputed to be over 5000 years old. The Common Yew can grow up to 65 feet and grows very slowly yet can form a dense hedge almost as quickly as any other species.

Other than Ivy, nothing will grow in the shade of a Yew, and almost all of its parts are toxic, with the exception of the flesh of its small red fruits – spit out the poisonous black pips. It is much feared by owners of prize stock.

Occuring naturally in woods and widely planted, male and female Yew trees are often to be found in churchyards where they predate the church.

The best timber trees are all extinct such was the importance of Yew in longbow manufacture, and later costly furniture. Now the twisted, gnarled wood can still be converted by craftsmen into objects of wonder.

The dense wood burns as well as coal.